Tales
from an Irish
Hermitage

Tales from an Irish Hermitage

Proceeds from this book go to feed the hungry and
clothe the naked. We thank you for your purchase.

To see some of our other products, go to
www.xanga.com/sistersofgraceofchrist

ISBN: 978-0-9809317-0-9

Tales from an Irish Hermitage

by a Nun of Grace

Table of Contents

Introduction

Nestling into the green-shawled breast on an Irish mountain a small hermitage hides…

Reached only by a bridge, it is girded on the other three sides by water... two fast-flowing streams and the wide, restless sea…

Trees shelter it lovingly… old native ash and alder, rowan and willow; hawthorn and fuchsia hedge it…

Here dwells a Nun, a Monastic Solitary, living apart from her Order in a work of cloistered Prayer.

She wears the full, traditional Monastic Habit of her Order. Full-length, black habit, deep blue scapular, white guimp and large white wimple. Her veil is long, deep blue, lined with white. In these modest garments, she is known and visibly a Nun wherever she walks... A Bride of Christ, walking always with Him.

The skills of her hands in her seclusion support the care of the homeless, especially children, in many lands where her Sisters in Christ Jesus live out their calling among the most needy of mankind...

Her outgoings are few, for essentials only, her visitors fewer. Her love for others expressed in her separation...

Hers are the seasons, the flowers and food she tends in her gardens... the wild flowers... Hers the first birdsong of the day, the last sweet vespers they linger in...

Hers too are the creatures who enrich her life... Those no one wants, like the little ones her Sisters care for... the lost, the sick, the crippled...

These tales are random... single threads in a rich tapestry of many years, taken from the pattern... Single flowers in a fair posy... They carry truth in them.

Inevitably then there is some overlapping, for lives intertwine always.

Beginnings and endings… endings and beginnings… Partings and meetings…

Chapter One

It was a winter's afternoon.

November, and the days shortening more
and more.

Rain danced and drummed on the small
windows of the hermitage, and the wind
sang its ancient melodies in the tall trees that
sheltered the old dwelling.

The fire burnt and glowed in the great old
hearth place. Turf, Irish incense, dug from
the high peat bogs, with a fragrant beech log
at its heart adding its sweet aroma.

It was an afternoon to stay indoors by the
fire, safe from wind and weather.

A day for knitting, and dreaming the hours
away.

And this is what Sister was doing.

Her fingers flew and her knitting needles twinkled.

At her side was a creel overflowing with wool of all colours and kinds, a rainbow of soft threads…

This was a skill she loved, and one she was delighted to be able to use now in her seclusion.

To help her Sisters to feed the hungry and clothe the naked in the Holy Name of Jesus in many lands.

For, like all the Sisters, she supported the work of her Order with the homeless, with an especial care for children.

In a week or so, Sister would take her work, the bright hats and mittens, thick, warm scarves and delicate lacy baby garments, to sell. With the rosaries she threaded, cards, home made preserves, and a gathering of other crafts, she would fill a stall at one of the local, thriving Farmers' Markets that were springing up around Ireland.

So few hand-knitted now, and she knew from her past experience that these pretty items would sell well, especially in the run-up to Christmas. Hand work was still prized here after all, and a vital part of local culture and tradition.

As she chose a new ball of yarn, her eyes fell on the old rug on the worn flagstone hearth… And she smiled.

Eight legs, two heads, two tails, yet the fluffy black and white furry ones were so intertwined it was hard to tell where one cat ended and the other began.

Thus these siblings had lived in the womb, and thus they slept still, in the glow of the fire, their fur too hot to touch, sprawled with their fluid feline grace.

Sister's latest rescued ones… half-grown yet, and full of affection and charm… and of sheer joie de vivre and energy.

The latest in a long, long line of critters that had come her way, knowing that here in this sheltered place they would find safety and love.

That here they would be protected from a harsh world.

Bringing their need and their love.

The wool Sister chose first was the classic cream Irish bainin, rich, soft locally spun… Straight from the sheep, grown on the green, green grass, weathered by the gentle rain and mountain winds…

A pure wool, native to Ireland.

She fingered it, her mind roaming back over the years, and as she cast on the cabled hat, she smiled at the memory it evoked...

Of fleece still growing, springy on the back of a wee, lost ewe who had sought her out…

Oonagh's Last Lamb

She gazed longingly through the old, stunted hawthorns and broken-down fence, across the wide ditch.

Where the ancient willows reclined gracefully and wild flowers flourished in the shelter of the boughs, each in their season. Violets, primroses… celandine gold and buttercup bright. Bluebells scattering the sky there.

Ripening into summer hues of rose and purple thistles and ragged robin.

She was a black-faced little mountainey sheep, with all the hardiness of her breed...

But now she was old.

The horns which had twisted around her face were crooked, and one had been cut back, giving her a quaint, lopsided look... And her bony muzzle was greying.

Spindly-legged now, and barrel-bellied with age.

Her golden eyes wise and knowing.

She had lived all her life on this mountain, and she knew every tree, every stone, every bend of the stream.

Where the hawthorn burst forth first into the delicious shoots of early spring, the bent old willows that a hot ewe, itchy in midsummer, ripe for the shearing, could wriggle under and scratch her fleecy back to her heart's content.

And she had borne many fine lambs, almost always twins, always in the same nest of shelter by the stream.

Surrounded always by her sister-ewes, and tended by the shepherd.

But now she was old.

And now she was alone.

All the rest of her flock had been taken off the mountain, she knew not where, in these bleak February days when the last of the grass in the worn-out pasture had been nibbled down to the roots..

Neglected land, choked with reeds and thistles.

But now she was old, and the farmer had shrugged his shoulders, driven her away from the flock, and left her on the mountain.

Obviously he thought she would bear no more lambs…

She was old.

She gazed longingly through the bushes..
Hungry, lonely… A wild creature tamed by
need.

And she watched Sister, who was filling a
bowl with the tasty sheep nuts they all
craved and adored in these winter days.

As one farmer said, the best "dog" in the
world was a bag of sheep nuts… Even the
wildest ram would follow anyone anywhere
for them, docile...

One of the first things Sister had seen in
Ireland was an old , bent man carrying a
plastic bag of these tasty morsels walking
along a country lane, with two huge rams
meekly following him.

She saw the fine big young ewe Sister had
had from birth greedily feeding from her
hands.

Smelled the sweet sheep nuts, her old
muzzle twitching.

11

There was still fine grass over the fence too; clean water, and a kind voice… another ewe…

Sister suddenly felt the intense gaze on her, and turned, her long blue veil swinging in the wind…

And her keen eyes met the yearning golden gaze of the little old ewe.

She frowned, puzzled. Surely all the sheep had been taken down the mountain a few days before?

She had heard the farmer calling them, seen the flock moving down the lane as she drove up…

Maybe this one had been in a far corner and the farmer had missed her?

It was unusual, as sheep followed each other.

And usually they were rounded up by the dog and carefully counted.

And in-lamb ewes were precious…

So she waited and watched.

Snow fell that night, and when Sister padded out at first light in her sturdy Wellingtons, her thick blue shawl wrapped firmly round her head and shoulders, to tend her ewe, there she was again.

The old one, grey against the pure dazzling whiteness of the virgin snow, waiting by the old car where the feed was stored.

Somehow she had breached the fence, come across the ditch?

Sister stopped in her tracks; this was a wild field sheep, not a tame pet like her ewe.

Yet she did not move as Sister approached.. not even when, quietly crisping through the virgin snow, she came within hand-reach of her.

And again, the two pairs of eyes met.

"Little sheep," Sister said quietly. "You are not mine. You belong to the farmer and he will be missing you. Maybe he has been up already looking for you, and here you are, not in his field. I will feed you of course, but then I must take you back to where he can find you…"

She was moved and amazed when the little ewe ate from her hand with no fear… Usually, you would put the food down and they would eat then, eyes always on you, unblinking, wary…

Awed when the old ewe let her rub her soft old muzzle.

Only the shepherd who was known to them was trusted. As Jesus tells us…

Just as her own ewe bleated loudly if any stranger approached the hermitage.

So she fed the little old ewe a generous measure of sheep nuts, then led her up to the gate and over the bridge. The ewe followed her meekly.

But the next day, there she was again, waiting by the old car... golden eyes alert, patient…

And again, Sister fed her, and again she took her up to the gate.

Looking at the old ewe, she was sure she was in lamb; but she saw too why there might be problems with the birthing…

The third morning, there she was again, coming eagerly to Sister and nuzzling her.

Three times now, and enough was enough.

Sister fed her, then went back indoors to make a couple of 'phone calls.

For in the village the day before she had learned that the land around her had been sold to "the forestry."

The man who had owned it had sold his sheep to a farm many miles away. Sister had listened and had said nothing.

She came out from the hermitage after making the calls, her face flushed with emotion.

But to the ewe, as she rubbed the old face, an old lady who had served and given all her life, she said simply,

"You are mine now, little ewe, and welcome to stay here with my ewe for as long as you live. No one will ever abandon you again...

"And no one will harm you, ever. Not ever. That is the promise to you... And we will call you Oonagh..."

And, Sister thought, the last laugh may well be on the farmer, as she was more sure than ever that there was a live lamb inside Oonagh.

Time would tell of course.

So the little old ewe joined the big tame ewe
in the wide, tree-shaded paddock... Always
she came and nuzzled Sister, fed from her
hand.

Gentle and grateful, a sweet old ewe...

And she even bore the initial jealousy of the
tame ewe patiently and with gentleness,
until the petted one became used to her.

Sheep, after all, are not solitary creatures by
nature.

But every day she would disappear for a
while—for mountainey sheep are great
leapers and very determined...

Sister would climb the fence and silently
seek her by the stream.

And always she would find her in the same
place, a flat bank, sheltered and shaded by
an old, recumbent willow tree that arched
protectively over a hollow.

Sister watched her as the weeks passed and as February ripened into March… And she was more sure than ever that Oonagh was in lamb…

She saw the spindly legged ewe widen, and the udder fill with milk…

March brought the daffodils to the hermitage, unfurling their golden skirts to join in the merry wind-dance of spring… Daisies starred the grass..

It was a warm, breezy March day, when the sky was blue and filled with scudding white clouds, when Oonagh did not at first come when Sister called her to feed.

Again she called, her heart in her mouth.

Always Oonagh, ravenously hungry with the increasing demands of the unborn lamb, came for food.

And then, wonder of wonders, the old ewe appeared from the trees, and behold! A tiny newborn lamb at her side. Perfect, the crisp coat still birth-wet… A little ewe..

Brand spanking new…

Trotting shyly along at her mother's side.

Sister's heart knew swift joy…

Oonagh had triumphed… and she would be a splendid mother to this lamb of her old age.

And here, in this sacred place, quiet and safe and set apart, she would be safe with her little ewe lamb.

And Sister's other pet ewe? Ah, that is a story for another day…

Chapter Two

Sister's nimble fingers wove the twisting cables swiftly and expertly, then shaped the top of the cap and pulled the last stitches together.

And added the work to the growing pile on the table, to be sewn up and finished later…

She stooped to add more turf to the fire, stroking the sleeping cats as she bent over them.

They stretched out on their backs, white bellies trusting her… Yet they woke not.

Now Sister selected more yarn… a soft yellow wool touched her fingers... Wool came in from many sources, and this was a synthetic of rare quality.

Perfect for baby wear…

As she raised it into the lamplight, she felt again the fluff of baby chicks...

She did not keep hens now.. well, not in the way she had done in past years… And the one chicken who had come her way in this Irish hermitage was not a fluffy newborn hatchling...

Yet the memory of this, her last encounter with a hen, was too poignant and too recent not to engage her quiet mind as she began the small booties…

The Hen With No Toes

One day during Lent, Sister visited a petting farm… She had seen signs to it and today she had time… and she was thinking of maybe once again keeping a few hens for the fresh eggs, and a secure coop for them against the predators that lived on the mountain.

Spring was near, and thoughts turned brightly to these plans and ideas for the coming summer.

And maybe he knew of a battery unit who were about to replace their laying stock? Sister could rescue a few of those birds then.

It was an idea never realized, for when Sister learned how many predators roamed these mountains, she decided that this was not for her here.

The land around the hermitage was full of trees and bushes, of places where a hen could hide and not be found at nightfall.

The farmer welcomed her and showed her round.

A wonderful place, with animals ranging free and happy… pigmy goats in the hay loft, a huge pink sow rolling in golden straw… chickens everywhere, and a reindeer in full antler gazing out from a stable door…

An overweight turkey he had on a diet, sharing a cage with a pure white dove that caught at Sister's heart.

Yes, he knew of a battery unit and he gave her the number, and yes, there was a coop she could have too.

Sister followed him into a dark shed to help him get it out, and suddenly…

"Sister! Can you save a hen with a bad leg?"

And a small black-feathered bundle with belligerent beady eyes was thrust at her.

Sister blinked.. "Well… my cat might eat her…"

"OK," and the hen was grabbed back...

"But she will have the coop…."

Sister's protective heart was engaged already, so she leaned over and took the scrawny hen back.

"She's been in here all winter to stop the others attacking her…"

Sister was intrigued… and, the coop loaded and lashed in the open tailgate of the small old car, they put the chicken in a crate on the passenger seat…

She would decide about more hens later.

Four sliced white loaves followed…

Chickens being chickens, Sister was soon very glad of the open tailgate… And chuckled at the feisty-eyed little bird who stared sideways at her all the way, clearly outraged and not about to enjoy the ride.

And once home, she put the coop on the grass in front of the hermitage so she could get the cats used to birds that were not to be chased and attacked..

And in went the hen…

Sister wanted her to settle before she looked at this " bad leg"...

She had already realized that the hen had spent so much time off her feet that her breastbone was bare, the dark feathers worn away there.

The wonder was that she had survived; usually when a hen goes off its feet, it does not live long.

So this little one was a fighter, a survivor, who deserved every chance thus.

As she was used to bread, in went a slice of the white bread—and Sister gazed open-mouthed as the hen demolished the bread at great speed, leaving just the ring of crust...

A few blades of grass, a long drink of water, and the hen settled down, still eyeing Sister sideways.

The cats had crept up and were sitting on the edge of Sister's habit...

Gazing unblinkingly at the new resident.

Hen was totally unfazed by this.

As early night fell, Sister worried about the wee hen out there all alone in the cold and frost... so she took out the big cat box, lined it with newspaper and dry grass, and in went the little hen for the night, inside the door…

In the early hours, she could be heard, softly crooning and singing to herself in the dawning day… a peaceful little melody.

That day, Sister picked her up to have a look at this "bad leg"...

And was appalled and puzzled. The little hen simply had no real feet! A couple of vestiges of toes, curled up, with a few stubby feathers poking out where no feathers should grow.

Was this hereditary, or injury?

Maybe it was better not to ask. She was painfully thin, but spirited, and not in any pain…

So the remedy was good food, sun and light, and company…

So that was the way it was.

Sister let her free in the day... When the cats tried to stalk her, as cats will, she fixed them with a beady stare and pecked them sharply on their sensitive noses.

Eyes smarting and dignity wounded, they backed off, pretended they had no interest in this creature, and never troubled her again.

Sister hid her laughter at the small drama.

And Hen swiftly made herself totally at home. The door was often open as the days lengthened and mildened, and she was to be found perching atop the door, nesting on the chairs, which often meant evicting the cats therefrom... Which she did with great aplomb...

Sister swiftly covered everything with newspaper in the day, for hens are not easy to house train. And it was easier thus than to keep the door closed.

When the door was closed, she would find her way onto the window ledge and stare in balefully, or try to get in through any open window.

And when Sister sat outdoors knitting, Hen would nestle under her chair, crooning and preening there.

As the weeks passed, the little hen grew sleek and put on weight. Her menu widened now, she ate voraciously, stealing from the cats' bowls.

Always a slice of white bread would be most zealously dealt with—interspersed with blades of grass as salad.

The feathers grew back on her breast… And somehow she moved fast, with a hoppity-skip and a dot and carry one…

And one memorable day, when food appeared at the door when she was far away, Hen found she could fly… Wheeeee! In she came, with a crash landing that made Sister wince. She scattered the cats in great alarm, but this worried Hen not at all.

There was no stopping her now.

Flight became her preferred mode of transport.

Why worry if your feet are bad if you can fly?

Sister wondered if she would lay? She was obviously part Bantam, part Black Rock.

Wild hens are seasonal… they are not full time layers like their artificially kept cousins. They lay only to reproduce, around a dozen eggs at two day intervals…

A clutch… and only if those fail will they lay a second clutch.

So when one morning Hen did not appear midmorning for food, Sister suspected what was happening. Quietly she sat by the door with her knitting, and watched and waited.

An hour passed thus, and another, the vigil patient in the warm sun, cats at her feet, as the blue baby booties grew and took shape…

Then her quick eyes caught a glimpse of black tail feather, and there was Hen, looking insouciant and innocent. And very pleased with herself.

Sister fetched her a slice of white bread, and, while Hen was thus engaged, went for a careful walk.

She spotted the bent grasses so neatly moulded by Hen's downy and determined breast, and gently caught up the small brown egg, still warm…

"Thank you, little Hen," she smiled… for it was, there being no cockerel, no use leaving the egg there. And a fresh egg, lovingly laid, would make a real treat…

And thus it went on that summer long... Eggs every few weeks.

Hen moulted in autumn, and the long winter passed quietly. Her routine remained the same; and she followed Sister and the cats wherever she went on the land.

She was an integral part of the hermitage family. Her morning song brightened the dark days...

A second spring, and a second summer, and Sister was out more than before in those months.

So when Hen disappeared, she was not followed, and Sister perforce allowed her to accumulate her eggs.

She realized too late that Hen was sitting seriously. Bantams are well known for their broodiness and excellent maternal instincts and often hen keepers will use one to hatch even goose eggs.

And if they are taken off their eggs, they will sometime pine and die...

So Sister let time pass.

One day she determined enough weeks had passed to allow Hen to realize deep in her small brain that these eggs were not going to hatch.

Hen had been coming for food every day, flying in at great speed.

"Cannot stay—eggs are there, feed me, give me water… let me stretch my legs a minute… must go now…" Then off she would flap again, hoppity skip, fly a while...

So this day, Sister made as if to follow the little black hen… Oh no; Hen was not having that! Oh dearie me no… No way was she about to allow her eggs to be stolen yet again!

So she went off in every direction, looking back to make sure she had distracted Sister from the right place…

Sister smiled, and simply followed a pace or three, then stopped and pretended to look elsewhere, to allay the wily bird's fears.

And from the corner of her eye, saw the general direction, waited a few minutes, then searched, quietly and carefully.

My, what a clever hen she had been. She was so near where the little old car was parked that you would never think to look there. Sister had searched further away and was about to give up when she almost stepped on the black hen.

She checked the eggs; shiny now with being brooded.

"Alright, little one. Tomorrow I will start to take the eggs away, a few at a time, and soon you will lose interest… Please God you are safe here now…"

Sister was out the following day, and it was evening before she came to start removing the eggs.

What she found brought tears to her eyes.

All that was there was a scrap of broken shell, and a few black feathers drifting in the long grass.

Hen had given her all for her eggs, for the chicks that would never be… She had laid down her very life…

And now she was part of the earth, part of the wind and the trees and the flowers, in this place where she had given so much delight and affection… Part of the very air now…

Leaving such sweet and poignant memories.

"Ah, Hen; never was there a bird like you and there never will be… I will never forget you—and now, nor will anyone else…"

Chapter Three

Was it the turf smoke that misted Sister's eyes?

No matter…

No sin to love.
No sin to cherish and care.

She worked on in the soft firelight, listening to the rain and wind...

Her mind roamed back in memory over the years to her time in a different hermitage, on a small, remote offshore island.

There, there had been no natural predators… no fox or weasel, or escaped mink to take a hen on her eggs…

She had been younger then, and it was a time when there was less need for her skills and her prayer to serve the work of those of her Sisters in active callings in far away lands.

So there she had lived a life of near self-sufficiency.

Always the Sisters grew their food when they could, starting gardens wherever they were…

Sister had taken this further, with a goat for milk and cheese, hens for eggs.

And, as a visiting Minister had put it, she had gathered a "menagerie" around her...

A couple of young Jacob's sheep, so she could spin their fleece… peafowl for the beauty and wildness of them… Ducks, geese…

The hermitage there had become a place of safety and peace, surrounded and protected by prayer…

Where no critter was abused or exploited, or eaten.

And there she had learned skills, of nurturing, or caring for the different ones on her land… of watching the wild ones too… that would never leave her…

Now, working the soft yellow yarn into pretty baby garments, her thoughts went back to fluffy chicks of many kinds…

Cheepy

Sister, in the second year of her hen keeping, had added to her small flock a few Black Rock pullets from a neighbouring farm...

And a very handsome young cockerel... Resplendent of plumage and proud of comb.

This latter had been rescued from certain death at the beak and talons of his father.

For when his first full year began, the old cockerel started attacking this rival savagely.

When he arrived at the hermitage, his comb and wattles were black with bruising.

The newcomers were already used to the outdoors and fiercely independent; no lap or shoulder birds these! Fine big birds; a neighbour assured her that they would lay "deep broon" eggs—as indeed they did.

Their plumage was black, with russet highlights. Their feet repelled... Black and scaly! Reminding of their reptilian ancestry.

Hens lay in all kinds of strange nooks and crannies, and are difficult to deter once they have chosen their nest.

And, as Sister knew well, they could infiltrate the most secure of gardens.

One of the new pullets insisted on laying in the flourishing bed of the striped ornamental grass under Sister's bedroom window.

Sister duly gathered in the eggs from there, as from other odd places. It meant keeping a sharp eye on the hens.

But it was a pleasant enough task, to wander alert around the garden and the field that ran sloping with its wide view over the sea in the early evening.

And deeply satisfying to come in with a basket of new-laid eggs…

After some weeks of this, this hen began to show all the signs of going broody.

Sure by now of fertile eggs, Sister gathered up a day's eggs at random from all her hens and arranged them neatly in the nest so carefully hollowed out and moulded in the grassy roots.

A clucking hen is a very valuable creature. Whether you want table birds or more chickens, this, after all, is the only way, even in this age of technological wonders, that you can get hens... Or eggs for that matter...

Oh, you can use an incubator, but it is just not the same...

It was comforting in those summer weeks, as Sister slept with the window wide open, to the sweet, wild night air, to hear the tiny chinking in the small hours as the black hen turned the eggs with that unerring and mysterious instinct.

The smell when you get close to a sitting hen is the worst in the world. Which is why you keep your distance. Which is the purpose of the smell... No self-respecting predator is going to go near something that smells so utterly foul... Another of the wonderful provisions in creation for the continuity of life...

Sister knew that when it comes to the hatching, untried hens are erratic and not always skillful. The idea of a tiny bird dying in the shell was unthinkable. And sometimes thus it is needful to assist the birth process.

The hen does not understand this… and her forceful peck can bruise. This hen was certainly fierce...

But Sister braved it at intervals on that hatching day... There were tiny black chicks; one had already been crushed to death against the unhatched eggs, so she carefully extracted those eggs that were still whole, leaving her to brood her three live chicks...

Indoors, she held the eggs to her ear and simply listened.

The sound of the tapping and tiny cheeping from inside an egg is a miracle you never weary of.

Over the next day and night, she carefully and delicately helped the chicks out, then returned them to the brood.

This at first confuses the hen, but she soon changes from hostility to nurturing.

There were then just a couple of eggs left. Sister was understandably reluctant to throw them out if there were any chance of life there.

So she gave them just one more night under the lamp (a small reading light with a flexible neck).

In the morning there was a faint tapping from one...

It was so faint that Sister judged the chick was in difficulties, so carefully cracked the shell. This is difficult; if you get the timing wrong the chick dies. If you leave it too late, the chick dies.

There is nothing quite so primeval as a hatching chick.

They lie curled so tightly in their nurturing shells, one huge claw over their head... Great bulging eyes. And still wet. No pretty fluffy creatures, until the breath of life has filled them out, and the air has dried their straggly covering.

This chick took so long to gather any strength; they have enough nourishment still in them from the yolk sac for about 48 hours. After a couple of days, he had rallied enough, it seemed, to be restored to his family.

Sister had no wish, dear as the new creature was, to adopt a tame chicken... and after two nights vigil, she needed sleep.

The chick was thoroughly delighted to go to his natural mother. Or, rather, his adopted mother?

For although the eggs had been gathered at random from the dozen motley hens, all the hatched chicks were black.

Except this one, who was a delicate, pale yellow...

Baby chicks grow so swiftly. His siblings were by now two days ahead of him, two vital days that are a long while in their little lives.

Sister, biting her lip, watched the saga unfold from the doorstep. The grass was long, where the hen was leading her chicks... Mother hen would find a tasty morsel, and call to them in that husky, throaty way. The black chicks would scurry to her. Devour the morsel.

And in the van, game, valiant, but hopelessly outrun, there would be the tiny yellow chick.

By the time he got there, the food was eaten, and the group was moving on to the next feed.

Sister of course tried to remedy this by feeding them. But every time, the story was the same.

The sheer spunk of that chick! He never gave up trying.

She deemed also that he would be fine and safe at night, tucked up with the others under the hen's downy breast.

And at first, this was indeed so.

But the mist and a soaking drizzle came in one night.

Sister was woken during the short summer night by a plaintive and incredibly loud cheeping... It went on and on, the epitome of terror and need.

So, of course, she emerged from her bed, and fetched a torch, and went out to the patch of grass where the nest was, in the heavy mist and saturating drizzle they call sea haar in those northern waters.

It took her a long time to trace the sound; she knew she was near, but just could not find the chick in the matted grass.

She was soon soaked to the skin… her sleeves sodden from parting the tangled stems of the grasses, a nasty, insidious chill…

And still no chick.

Eventually the torch beam fell on this tiny yellow, bedraggled scrap of fluff, firmly wedged in a tuft of grass.

Sister painstakingly disentangled him, and carried him carefully in her cupped hands into the kitchen, where the box and lamp still stood at the ready.

He was soaked!

Gently she dried him on tissue, then laid him on sweet dry grass under the lamp. He was shivering so hard he kept falling over, poor scrap...

All she could do now was pray, and leave him to recover, if that was within him… And seek warmth and dry clothes for herself.

In the morning there he was, cheeping away, full of life and joy, ready for food and milk...

She knew from past experience that if she were not careful, she would end up with what one old lady called "a very silly chicken."

But she had said it with such affection and fond memories that it had clearly been a happy experience...

And what choice here?

Left outside, this brave wee bird would simply die.

A pattern thus emerged; every morning Sister would put him outside with the other chicks, then at night she needed to bring him in for safety.

He took a few days to recover fully from his soaking, and every morning she would peep into the kitchen, heart in her mouth, expecting to find a pathetic little corpse.

And every morning there would be the sunshine of his enthusiastic cheeping to greet her.

Sister had until then had no idea of how wide a chick's verbal repertoire is; they have a song all of their own. "I am ALIVE! I love life! Isn't it wonderful? BE HAPPY!"

There are trills and scales, a veritable aria of song!

And this tiny creature's joi de vivre and enthusiasm were so infectious.

Oh, Sister went on making very sincere efforts to keep him in his chicken world...

After a couple of weeks, she decided it was time the chicks were in the safe coop behind the hermitage with the other hens.

Safe there from the depredations of the great black-backed gulls who would swoop in for small chicks.

Their depredations on her beloved flowers and the precious vegetables were getting very serious.

So she gathered them up in a bucket, seized the squawking hen under her arm, and carried them round to the coop, closing and fastening the door very carefully.

This, she reasoned, was after all better for Cheepy. He was bigger now and she could still keep a close eye on him...

Sister never, ever could discover how Cheepy escaped from the coop. None of the other chicks managed it.

But there he was at the back door, cheeping indignantly...

Yes, Sister now had a very, very silly chicken... attached and bonded to her… And she was charmed and delighted at this awesome responsibility...

Motherhood is to be taken very seriously, you must realize. Here she was, now the sole supporter of a frail and tiny chick...

That summer there were long periods of clear skies and hot sunshine. The sounds and smells of those sweet fragrant months lingered long in Sister's memory.

The hay crop was rich and dry, the workers passing the hermitage as they went from farm to farm. The scent of the sweet grass filled the air, mingling with the sea breeze.

Wherever she went in garden or field, Cheepy came too, following her closely.

When she rested on a blanket in the afternoons, he snuggled up in the crook of her elbow, crooning and chirping.

His happiness revolved around being as close to her as possible.

When she worked at the garden, weeding the flower borders with a trowel, Cheepy thought this was solely for his benefit. After all, this was behaviour he understood with every chicken instinct. The mother hen scratching for food for him...

When she had been to the village, he would run flapping to greet the car, ecstatic, and perch on her arm like a falcon.

When she got up in the morning, he was on the doorstep; if she was late, he would cheep indignantly.

When a tiny creature attaches itself limpet-like to you, it reaches to your very soul.

His total dependence, emotionally and physically, awed and delighted.

As his feathers grew in, ungainly adolescent phase of stubby quills, it was clear he was going to be pure white, a throwback to some distant ancestor...

All was sheer beauty.

But summers end.

When he grew very big, Sister deemed it fairer to accustom him to life with the other chickens.

A fully grown cockerel inside the house was a daunting thought... especially when his voice came in…

So, into the back he went. There was some initial pecking from the other hens, who take time to get used to strangers in their midst, but this soon resolved.

And until the following spring, the cockerel would not see him as a threat.

So there was a respite.

It was, of course, so hard to let him go like this...

After a while Sister really thought Cheepy had totally forgotten her… and that was not easy!

Then one day as she was collecting kindling in the copse, there he was, scratching around by her hands, with that old expression in his eyes, wanting to be tickled...

He was huge, a fine white cockerel, and Sister was so proud of him...

But winter came early that year, with a wet, cold, stormy spell at the end of October.

One day Cheepy was limping badly.

The next day there was no white cockerel out there, and Sister's heart nearly stopped.

In the wild wind and rain, she searched for him once again, as she had that first time, so long ago.

And again, she found him, behind the shed, unable to walk, and again, she carried him carefully indoors.

And again, she placed him lovingly in a cardboard box in the kitchen, with sweet dry hay, a pot of milk and a dish of food.

And a hot water bottle well wrapped and tucked under the hay...

Cheepy was ecstatic at this! Cheeping and eating greedily!

Sister tried again and again to get him to walk, but to no avail this time.

And she knew what the outcome would be. There was nothing more she could do.

And one morning she came into the kitchen, to a stillness.

It is a strange and unmistakable quietness, this absence of life when death has visited.

Cheepy was there, head under his wing. He had simply fallen asleep...

Sister buried him, misty-eyed and unashamed of her tears, in the sheltered patch just outside the garden looking out over the sea, with wild fuchsias bending over, and the sweet birdsong and moonlight.

Probably he was never in nature's way "meant" to live; there was a weakness, a flaw, which is why he needed help even to hatch.

But he had such a blissfully happy little life! Just four months, and he had given so much in that time, of joy and of love.

Not a bad record for an egg...

Chapter Four

Sister was smiling now at the poignant memories, softened as they were by the years between…

She cast off the booties and began the matching hat, still the fluffy yellow yarn flying through her fingers…

There had been so many hens, so many hatchings… Yet some stood clear of the many…

Some brought more than memories of the birds themselves... of a different way of life.

Of the interaction with people from different backgrounds and cultures that is not easy.

Of ways of coping with this without doing damage.

Yet without compromising ideals and standards.

A Tale of Three Cockerels

By the time Sister had lived three years on the island, she had gathered a varied flock of hens… many were the offspring of her first birds now. All known to her, for chickens too are individuals with their own character and quirks.

There were, you see, no predators there… no foxes or weasels... so hens could be totally free range by day and night.

Only the chicks needed protecting from the great black-backed gulls...

So it made keeping hens easy.

The hermitage had land, a wide field on this island where no trees grew, windswept and bare.

Plenty of pecking for all there… and edged by the drainage ditches that were an essential in this place of heavy rains… and a low-lying part of the land often filled to make a natural pond.

The garden, filled with flowers and vegetables, was carefully fenced off, but still sometimes an aerial approach availed an ambitious hen seeking luxurious and private nesting for her precious brood.

For the hens often chose to lay and hatch their eggs in true natural fashion, spurning the laying boxes so carefully provided.

Sister learned then to watch where they were… always she knew and always she kept a weather eye.

There is, of course, no way to predict the sex of unhatched chicks, and on any farm there can only be one cockerel.

Apart from the noise (they challenge each other, and the cockerels on nearby farms by crowing back and forth, at a high rate of decibels) they will fight to the death, interbreed etc.

The usual "remedy" for spare cockerels in this "women's lib" setting is "the pot."

Sister was not in favour of this in any way. These were birds she had nurtured lovingly… and her hermitage had become thus a sanctuary, a quiet oasis where no creature was used for meat.

That left her free to care and love these little ones. To enjoy their company for their own sakes.

Once and once only had she allowed a neighbour to come and take away the spare cockerels.

Sister had felt obliged to catch and pen them, as this can only be done at night by literally knocking them off their perches in the dark.

And they scream! Oh, the noise they make... heartrending...

That one and only time, Sister, flustered and agitated, found herself comforting the distressed birds… "It's OK: no one is going to..." then stopping, realizing what was to happen.

In the morning early, she called the neighbour to cancel the arrangement…

Aware that they would call her soft, and not caring.

She knew the harsh history of this place, how hard the struggle for survival itself had been for these hardy folk, cut off and far from shops… Reliant totally on what they could grow and raise.

A beached whale provided great riches then for food and fuel, and seals were a bounty of food also.

The diet in winter was sparse... oats, potatoes, herring...

A cow going dry was a major disaster.

And few ever left the island.

But things were different now... There was a daily ferry from the mainland, food was in abundance... while the old culture had its attractions, subsistence farming was a thing of the past.

And Sister was not island-raised... so why should she torment herself by striving to adapt to the customs of past ages?

Let her birds live then!

To do else would spoil all her pleasure and delight at hatching time...

But this, of course, did not solve the problem of the overpopulation of cockerels.

Sister lay awake at night pondering and agonizing. There was no one she could even give these three to, as all who kept poultry were in the same situation.

And in a very short time, when spring came, these three youngsters would come into full fledge as cockerels. And her fine cockerel would attack them in no uncertain terms.

It was as she paced the shore one day that an answer came to her… she was poking around in the great heaps of seaweed that were washed ashore in the winter storms. Her nose wrinkled at the sight of the maggots that infested the smelly piles.

How her hens would love that feast, she thought… then stopped in her tracks as the harsh wind buffeted her, and slowly smiled.

She had the answer to her dilemma…

And so it was that late one night—and Sister had the great advantage as a Monastic of keeping different hours from the rest of the islanders, who were all fast asleep in their beds—she emerged from the hermitage, torch and big stick and sack in hand.

She crept to the big barn where the hens roosted, flashed the torch quickly to see who was where, and, her heart racing, skillfully knocked a cockerel off his perch.

Speed was of the essence, else the whole flock would panic and there would be no more catching for several hours.

Cockerel number two was un-perched and bagged...

Screaming loudly of course, and Sister holding her breath as she waited for the birds to settle a wee while, in case a neighbour had heard...

But there had been a dance at the hall the previous evening and the drink flowed at these occasions.

So all was quiet.

By now there was total chaos, the birds flustered and flying everywhere, dropping off the perches all around her.

"No one is going to harm you," she softly assured them, gleeful and relieved that this time it was true.

And when the birds had settled a little, she located the third cockerel, and with the screams ringing in her ears, he too was safely bagged.

And in the pearl grey of the early morning, sacks wriggling in the back of the car, and singing a happy hymn, Sister drove to the shore where the seaweed was heaped and where maggots crawled for the eating.

There was a ruined cottage there, so shelter for them… and fresh rainwater in abundance. Perfect…

And with huge satisfaction Sister watched the three renegades lope off into the dawn... Wished them well and farewell.

And made her quiet way home for early prayers and welcome coffee... well pleased at her night's work...

For various reasons, Sister did not get back to the shore for some weeks after that. There was heavy snow for one thing, then she caught a cold....

One of the Sisters who she had mailed the story to wondered if folk would see the cockerels and guess their origin.

Sister knew these people and laughed. "Probably—but no one would dare accuse me to my face!"

We also wondered if they might "home"— but Sister thought not.

Hens new to the hermitage never showed any inclination to roam in search of past dwellings. Food and shelter was all they sought in their simplicity.

It was a few weeks later that the neighbour who had been originally asked to cull the cockerels rang Sister.

Such a call was a very rare event, and Sister was still recovering from her bad cold, so was not as alert as she might have been.

"Have you been down to the shore recently?"

Sister explained she was ill, but she realized that her words had gone unheard.

That emotion was running so high all she could do was let the words come out…

"So you haven't seen those three roosters someone's put there, running about?"

Sister was very thankful she didn't have videophone! Her first reaction, stifled just in time, was delight and relief. The "boys" were safe!

"NEVER!" she exclaimed realistically, chuckling inwardly—and knowing full well the neighbour knew they were hers.

"CRUEL that," the neighbour opined, self-righteousness in every syllable...

(AND PULLING THE NECKS OF TERRIFIED BIRDS IS KIND?)

"There's no food for them there."

It was then Sister in her joyful tiredness made an unguarded mistake.

"Oh, I don't know! The seaweed is FULL of maggots..."

She bit her lip, but too late... the words were out…

You could have heard a pin drop...

A few nights later Sister saw, through her uncurtained window, torchlight flashing...

No car, just the lights. This, in her isolated situation there (the nearest house was about a quarter of a mile away) was very unusual.

But it was Saturday night, when the drink flows freely here and wise maidens stay put.

As day dawned, the peace was shattered and rent by many crowings and chasings...

The boys were back!

They patently did not want to be; they took off across the fields every time Sister appeared.

Even while quite desperate about all this, Sister noticed how fit and well they looked!

Any resemblance to a pampered barnyard cockerel had vanished in their months of freedom. They had reverted to the wild, and adapted beautifully, and she marveled and rejoiced to see them.

These were wild creatures, long of leg, small of body, fleet and wary.

Obviously the life suited them!

But they must have taken some catching…
She watched them legging it across the
fields, then drifting back to the nearest
house… The hermitage…

That day was one Sister would not easily
forget... The noise outside; four cockerels...

And her dilemma... They knew those birds
had come from here. By now the whole
island would have heard the tale.

So no way now could she even get them
culled in the traditional way.

And there was no one she could ask to help
either, or even tell anyone her trouble to.

So the long hours passed.

And a plan formed, for Sister was not going
to be beaten back, outmaneuvered, thwarted
in her mercy plans.

Her motives and her actions were pure and of strength.

And she had a distinct tactical advantage over these folk in that she slept little and at unusual hours.

It had stood her in good stead that first time, and it could do so again.

So, soon after midnight, there was Sister again, torch, pole, sacks... energised by need, furtively creeping through the mud, watching for lights going on across the fields...

My word they were stronger! And LOUDER! They fought and struggled... One sack "hopped" across the yard...

Sister was laughing and out of breath by the time they were all safe in the back of the old car.

And off she drove in the still, dark, blessedly solitary night...

Not this time to the shore…

The island was small, about six miles by
two, sparsely populated and wild. The shore
had simply been too confined a space.
And too many folk walked there, and there
were the fishermen too.

So now Sister drove clear across the island
to the wild, overgrown part that surrounds
and abuts on the tiny airstrip, used only once
a week.

By one of the ruined chapels she stopped,
hefted out the struggling sacks, and, one by
one, released the trio once more into the
sweet, clean air of freedom...

With huge satisfaction...

That was on Mothering Sunday, English
time, mid-Lent...

And there were never any calls, any reported
sightings…

Maybe if they were seen, the ones who saw were wise enough and wary enough to say nothing... maybe they even smiled secretly at the Sister who refused to be bullied.

For a small island set in a wild ocean sets its own rules and keeps its own counsel on many matters.

And no wild cockerels returned to haunt the hermitage.

And every year from then on, the hatchings were a joyful time... for no matter what sex these tiny ones were, they would be safe from sudden death... for next spring, they will join their siblings, living free in this fair and fertile land...

It might be a short life—but a blessed one… and much, much longer than others would have planned for them…

Chapter Five

Again, Sister reached into the turf creel to replenish the fire… soon she would have to go out to the shed to refill it, but there was enough for now.

Again, she caressed the hot fur, and again the cats stirred but woke not…

And her thoughts in memory plucked one more from her store of young birds… and again, her fingers flew through the soft yarn…

Gozzle the Lonely Gosling

The coming of the geese to the hermitage
was quite an event…

They arrived by the afternoon boat and then
in the back of a Landrover in a large
cardboard box, and the hot air that emerged
from the ventilation holes was awesome.

Two geese and a gander…

To prevent any escape bids while they were
acclimatizing—and the story of the homing
hermitage ducks is one for another day—

they were released, indignant and noisy, into a pen.

Almost everyone you asked about geese could tell you how at one time they had been chased by these large aggressive birds… and Sister ruefully remembered as a child being chased and held at bay atop a stock of bales of hay…

So she talked gently to them, fed them bruised barley and bread… maybe if she befriended them there would be no hostility.

The goat was affronted and in her jealousy went on milk strike for two days…

The ducks and hens were curious and surrounded the newcomers…

Who made very unfriendly hisses at them.

"Oh, DEAR!" murmured Sister. " I can see trouble ahead!"

After three days, she opened the pen door and stood away to let the geese emerge in their own time… thinking it would take a wee while.

In fact the gander exploded into the field, scattering hens and ducks...

The geese were gentler and more… genteel... Treading elegantly out…

Sister watched the riot, then quietly withdrew to let them sort the pecking order out… There was plenty of room for everyone, she reasoned, and the hens and ducks were faster and could seek refuge in smaller places…

Feeding time was interesting indeed… but she scattered the barley in enough places to outwit all.

That was when she experienced the aggression of the gander… He literally charged towards her, loud hissing, tongue out, long, thick neck outstretched, wings spread out…

Her response was instinctive; she knew that how she reacted now would colour the future of her small family!

The feed bucket was in her hand, so yelling as loudly as she could she belaboured the gander round the neck and body…

The result was electrifying and dramatic… after a few minutes, the gander ceded defeat... and never again did he attack or threaten the gentle Sister.

Which added greatly to her reputation locally as a charmer of animals…

As she said when asked, "There are some things in this life that I am afraid of... a gander full of hot air is not among them."

So, order and peace were restored… the geese had their territory, which all others respected… the goat forgave Sister for bringing in yet more critters, as she assured her she was loved… so milk flowed free again…

And in due time, as the spring finally ripened on the far northern island, the gentle geese started to lay their great white eggs.

Sister was fascinated; they laid like most birds, on alternate days, and on the evening of the no-egg day, the soon-to-be-laid egg lay low in their bellies, veiled yet visible.

And one egg made a whole meal… Boiling from cold for eight minutes produced a perfect soft-boiled egg with a deep orange yolk.

From her farmer-neighbours, she learned why hens were often used to hatch goose eggs. Simply, geese were not always reliable or steadfast in their month-long vigil.

A good clucking hen would stay the course…

So she set four eggs under a loud bantam, and let the goose sit herself also.

The first clutch under the hen yielded only one gosling, and that baby lived only a few days.

By now Sister was as used to this as she would ever be... she marveled at the golden coat of the tiny one… it was not the fluff of a chicken, but as waterproof fur…

Meanwhile she had set a second clutch, again under a hen… the geese were being true to their reputation and were not sitting tight enough.

On the due day, there was just one egg ticking… she waited a few hours, then as the tapping was getting fainter, she decided to intervene.

So this little gosling hatched under the lamp…

Alert and alive and so healthy she swiftly gave it back to the hen.

She had heard about how geese and ducks imprint on the first living creature they see.

He thrived out there. Growing apace, the hen was soon hard put to sit on her large offspring.

It was a comical sight, watching the hen trying to brood this ungainly chick.

Of course, he was definitely a chicken… and Sister was very special to him always… often as he grew, he would be heard almost wailing until she appeared.

Soon, the yellow waterproof fluff gave unsightly way to his true coat of pure white feathers… a bizarre mix at first, then day by day into a splendour…

One day Sister heard a great commotion from him… And found him distraught and alone…

That was when she realized why geese are aggressive. Although she was very near, Gozzle simply ran into her legs... Because she was standing still, he did not see her... it

was movement they saw and attacked...
Short sighted…

And he was bereft because the hen, weary of
her care and thinking that by now this bird
must be able to flutter with her into the
rafters, had gone back to roosting high...

After all, there was no way she could brood
this great ungainly creature any more. She
had had enough! No more!

So Gozzle had lost his mother... On whom
he had imprinted.

His cries echoed round the quiet field…

And of course, it was Sister he attached to
now in his distress.

She who he followed.

But from that day Gozzle's life in the field
went downhill, and there was nothing Sister
could do to alleviate his lost loneliness.

For geese are social creatures.

And no one wanted him…

He would try to attach to group after group...

But the ducks, who were white like him and had webbed feet like him, did not want him. They quacked at him and waddled away.

The hens squawked and flew to their roosts when he tried to join them…

They most certainly did not want him.

And the geese surely and truly did not want him! He was just not one of them.

The gander made that very clear... after all, a young drake? Oh NO!

That would never do.

So Gozzle would trail after group after group, crying and ungainly and… lost.

He had this identity crisis and nothing helped him.

Sister would watch from the window, her heart aching for him.

Whenever she went out, he would flap and waddle over to her, snaking his long, beautiful neck on her legs, adoring her, eating from her hand.

As she walked the land, there he would be, close on her heels...

And when she went indoors, he would start wailing until darkness brought him rest.

This would not do...

Much as Sister loved this great, beautiful, affectionate bird, who honoured her with his trust, she knew that he could not stay there beyond the winter...

By spring, he would become a full gander, and they would fight to the death.

And the usual solution to extra males made her shudder. No way could she eat Gozzle –

or send him to market where his fate would be the same…

Any mention from the neighbours of Christmas dinner made her shudder.

So she started seeking a new home for her baby…

And on a neighbouring island, there was a lady who felt as she did about animals and birds…

To whom they were pets to be cherished, never eaten.

This lady had geese... and the same breed as Gozzle… and she had a young female without a mate.

Called Ludmilla.

Anyone who gave her geese beautiful names was absolutely right by Sister.

So one fine autumn morning as the dew lay heavy on the grass, making filigree beauty of cobwebs, Sister determinedly coaxed her trusting gosling into a large crate and took him to the pier for the early boat.

It was not easy, but there we are.

She stood alone on the pier then, in the freshening wind, watching the ferry boat diminishing in size as it wound its slow way around the scattered islands.

"God bless and prosper you, sweet Gozzle! You gave me so much; long may you live in peace and freedom with your new mate."

Chapter Six

Sister stretched and leaned back against the chair, the baby set all done and joining the cabled cap and other small garments…

As if in harmony, the cats stretched and opened sleep-dazed eyes...

And Sister realized that the rain had ceased, and the wind had dropped as the short afternoon neared its ending.

There was peace and silence now.

It was often thus; and often too at the dawning the weather would change, from rain to clear, or from clear, starry skies to cloud and wind.

She glanced at the clock… time to refill the turf creel... time to walk a while in the sweet, rain-washed air… time for Vespers then, and to eat her simple evening meal.

The cats followed her to the door, and she laughed at their eagerness to be outside. Knowing they would follow her on her walk…

She took her big black cloak from its hook on the back of the door, donned waterproof boots, and out they went, the three of them.

The early evening light was clear, clean, pure…

"We won't go far," she told the cats, whose faces were lifted to her. "Just to the bottom of the copse, to stretch our legs…"

First there were the ewes to check and feed, so she filled a plastic bag with sheep nuts from the bin in the outbuilding, and set off for the paddock.

The woolly trio, their winter fleece rich and thick, ran to her, eager for food.

As she watched them eat, butting the cats away as they tried to invade the paddock,

Sister was thankful for the assistance of the petting farm man with them.

He had been so impressed with the long life Hen had enjoyed in her care, and deeply sympathetic when Oonagh came.

So now it was he who did the heavy work of shearing and checking feet for her. Enabling her thus to keep her pets.

Their manger filled, she resumed her stroll, calling the cats to follow her.

So they wound their way down the narrow twisting path that led through the trees and bushes.

All were bare now, stark in outline… Yet the swellings of the buds of the next leaves were there, clear to fingers and eyes.

And the furled, hard catkins dangled from the alders…

And the holly was sleek and shiny, the red berries still there…

There was a drift of darker fruit over the low hawthorns, and the white flowers of the ivy gleamed softly.

Reminding of Christmas not too far ahead...

Down Sister walked, enjoying the air and exercise... the cats followed, with an occasional diversion to race up a tree...

But always they rejoined her.

And down to the wooden gate that marked the beginning of the track to the beach...

"No, that is too far today," Sister decided. "We will just rest here a while together."

And she sat on the small bench that rested by the gate... gazing at the calm ocean lower down... resting eyes and mind on its eternal secrecy and peace...

Deep in the silent prayer that was her soul-food.

And then, stretching and settling the cats warm on her lap, letting memory take her yet again…

Seal Magic

The small hermitage where Sister lived had its own small beach, where she loved to walk...

A steep, narrow path led down from the hermitage, meandering through a small wood, and out through a wooden gate.

She emerged then into a wild and lonely place, where sea meets land, unspoilt, clean. The pale sand, wet from the outgoing tide, is fretted with the tiny footprints of a myriad birds, strewn with tiny shells.

Boulders lie there, heaped as if strewn by a giant hand, smoothed by centuries of sea times, draped with strange seaweeds… Periwinkles and all manner of mussels and other crustaceans clung to them.

And the sky is vast; always huge and never twice the same. Evanescent moods, changing, pulsing as the sea... Living... Cloudscapes, dramatic, blue stretching out on rare smiling days of summer. Heavy, leaden, in gale-stormed winter...

Seals bask there in great numbers on the rocky, seaweed-covered skerries at low tide.

They said that if you whistled, the seals would come.

They are, you see, very curious creatures, and still relatively unafraid.

Sister could not whistle and singing did not seem to have the same effect.

So, for many months, she had to content herself with these distant views.

They are, she quickly learnt, incredibly noisy creatures. There is a raucous symphony of grunts and barks playing... In the still, clear air in calm weather small sounds carry.

On one pilgrimage to the shore, Sister walked gently along, joying in the air and the wide, wide sky, and the sheer freedom. And singing thanks and praise to Jesus, as was her solitary wont.

Suddenly, she had that unmistakable awareness that she was being watched... Stopping, she looked around. There was no one to be seen, and there were no bushes here to conceal anyone...

This beach was private, inaccessible save from the hermitage.

Her puzzled gaze then turned to the sea— and close in to shore were a good number of huge-eyed, whiskered faces. The seals had come to listen to her thanksgiving "concert."

It made an already wondrous occasion totally enchanted... She sat there on the sand and sang... And the heads came closer; tails appeared too as they settled and relaxed... And when she finally tore herself away it was with a very full heart.

This was the beginning of a rich time for her... Slowly as she watched, she came to know individual seals... one that was paler than the others used to come nearer than the rest… Almost white, like the babies, but adult.

Frequently when she went down to the shore, there was not a seal in sight, especially at higher tides when the skerries where they bask are submerged.

But she had only to call, or begin to sing, and all the sleek, whiskered heads would emerge, coming close in to shore.

Their dark liquid eyes limpid.

Often, on cold, windy days, they lie with just their whiskered snouts visible, pointing skywards. Warmer thus...

Sister's outings then would be short, muffled in her big cloak against the piercing wind.

Often she would wait a while before she called them, hardly able to believe they would really respond to her voice, these wild creatures of deep oceans.

She knew of the troubles they had, of the accusations that they stole fish... that there were attacks on them… dark deeds on dark nights. For although these gentle creatures are protected in law, they are vulnerable still.

There is, if well-managed, plenty for us all —and oh, the loss, if these wild, free creatures of God were destroyed.

And for Sister, the most exciting and magical time was then yet to be.

Something she had never expected...

One day in early November, she went along the right side of the shore, rock-stepping as she loved to do. The huge rocks are bright and varied in their colours, smooth from aeons of tide-tossing...

Many are also very slippery, so she was proceeding very cautiously, and totally engrossed in her feet.

It was thus a considerable shock when the rock she was about to step onto snarled and moved... and she found herself gazing into the huge, liquidly dark eyes of a baby seal...

She could not believe it! This was an answer to unuttered prayer, to see one of these creatures so close.

And oh, he was even more beautiful than she could have imagined... Pure white fur, sleek and soft-looking.

And his mouth more full of vicious-looking teeth than she would have thought possible!

The teeth came as a considerable shock to Sister. She had not known such cuddlesome creatures owned them.

Retreating to the bank, she debated what to do; here, in this sheltered private cove, he was safe from attack.

But had he been abandoned? Would he survive? She had not realized the size of these babies! Or their fierceness; those teeth are formidable.

She decided, wisely, that she did not know enough to deal with this situation. So she trekked back up the path to the hermitage and called a local seal rescue organization…

From whom she learned so much.

As she told them when they asked, there were two adult seals in the water nearby. So it was likely that there was no immediate problem. Apparently baby seals do not go into the water for the first two weeks, so this was probably a newborn. Certainly there was not a speck of black on that glorious white coat. That, too, changes after a couple of weeks.

She was advised to keep an eye on it. And to call again if there was any concern.

That evening, and very early the following morning, Sister went down to the shore again; the seal had moved a couple of hundred yards along the rocks. The two seals were still there in the water just off the shore.

Their mobility is amazing. They look, with no feet, so ungainly. All they can do is rock.

Their tails are almost prehensile, expressive, with digits, levering them along effectively enough, but slowly, on their reluctant land journeyings.

And once in the water! Their speed and agility!

Watching them leap and dive with a reckless zest and freedom joys, and tugs at the heart.

Later that day, Sister went down again, as the tide was coming in.

At first she thought the baby was dead, and her heart misgave her… then when she came near, he woke up suddenly...

It was a mild, quiet day, so, intrigued, she hid behind some rocks, made herself comfortable and invisible, and kept very, very still.

So still that a tiny, neat, dapper wren all but landed on her shoe.

The mother seal kept looking for him, coming out of the water at different places... Finally she seemed to realize where he was, and simply kept vigil.

When the incoming tide touched the baby seal, he set up a loud, distressed-sounding wailing, an eerie and soul-rending sound.

Immediately the mother surged out of the water—only to be knocked back by the bigger seal. This intrigued and puzzled.

When the water was high around the baby, the mother came out and began to suckle him.

All this was a very few feet from where Sister lay, cloak-shrouded, in rapidly growing darkness. It was a sharing in something so intimate, almost holy.

And it was then she left, as the night made all invisible.

* * *

It was a wild, stormy night, and first light saw her anxiously struggling against the wind back to the shore.

The tide was very high, and there were the seal and its mother; the baby was trying to get out of the water, hard up against the rocks, and looked in distress.

So Sister went back to call again… And filled in the huge gaps in her knowledge, as the founder of the seal sanctuary himself answered the 'phone.

Listening to him talk was wondrous. His love and expertise shone out.

Apparently the bigger of the two waterborne seals was the bull; after mating, the fertilized eggs lie dormant for three months. So the bull was trying to mate with the mother—as she was seeking to nurture her existing pup.

As Sister had read, seal milk is very rich in fat. She was able to assure him that the baby was not injured, and was well-covered and vigorous.

He told her too, that, as she had surmised, some seal pups get "rescued" when, as with this one, they are fine... She had, thankfully, done the right thing...

She only saw the pup once more, then it vanished back into the sea, hopefully to grow strong and well.

The seals are a part of this place; it is, simply, theirs. Not ours. There is a children's song, haunting, poignant: "Think of a world without any flowers."

And Sister, on her walks to the shore, thought often thus about these huge, gentle and playful creatures, caught in time between sea and land. Without them, it would be a cold and barren world indeed.

They give a timeless, eternal dimension to a world that is racing too fast—draw us back to the slow and healing rhythms of God. Remind us of realities that are too easily ignored else.

And, even when the weather storms prevented her going to that wild, free place, Sister's heart and soul knew, as she sat by the fire listening to the wind howl, that they are there, living as God made them.

"Yonder is the great and wild sea with its living things too many to number, creatures both great and small... All of them look to you to give them their food in due season... You give it to them; they gather it; You open

Your hand, and they are filled with good things." (Psalm 104:26, 28-29)

Chapter Seven

Darkness had stolen in around the small group resting by the old wooden gate.

Sister sat on a while, the cats curled on her lap, twined together in their way… Their bodies warmed her...

Letting the peace fill her and surround her, praying thanksgiving in her quieting soul.

The beauty around her never failed to peacen and renew her.

The ocean gleamed still in the light of the rising moon, never still…

Above her, the sheltering trees rustled their bare branches gently…

"Time to go home," she reluctantly told the cats, tipping them carefully off her lap.

As they trekked back up the path, she plucked a few twigs of the alder catkins…

Maybe in the warmth, they would swell and open, and, even as they were, they were a welcome decoration for her small Oratory…

The hermitage greeted them, opened its warm shelter to them, and Sister went about her evening chores quietly…

The turf creel was refilled, more small logs brought in… the fire banked high for the evening…

Food for the cats… water too…

A check of the hermitage, a last walk round the inner gardens…

As she moved towards the door to go back in for the evening, a movement in the bushes caught her eyes.

She knew this well; it held no puzzlement or fears for her.

It was part of her surroundings now.

Another small friend out there in the night…

"Eat well, little one," she called, leaving bread and fruit on the step as she left the outdoor folk to their night work…

Recalling the meeting with this one…

The Night Visitor

It was early January, the first winter Sister lived up on the mountain.

Dark nights, cold and wet...

One night, as she was snug, drifting off to sleep, the cats on her bed as usual, a sound pulled her sharply awake... a rustling, scrabbling...

There had been mice and worse in the old cottage when Sister moved in. It had, after all, lain empty a while, and the wild creatures lived undisturbed then. And who could blame them? The hermitage was way up in the Irish mountains, a mile or more from the nearest house, hidden and sheltered.

A safe place for wild critters to live and flourish.

But the cats were good hunters, and soon the scratchings of tiny feet in the loft space and the walls were no more heard. There was peace in the night.

Sister lay still a moment, fully awake now, listening. There it was again… Something alive was in the sitting room… She ran her hands over the furry heads… all there.

"OK," she whispered. "Over to you…"

But the cats seemed suddenly heavy, glued to the bed, refusing to move even when she pushed them.

Hmmm. This was interesting indeed.

Silently, Sister crept carefully from the bed… Not a whisper; not a murmur…

Then she tripped over her slippers…

Sighing, she made her way to the sitting room.

And snapped on the light, knowing that whatever had been there would have fled at her carelessness.

Sure enough, the room was empty…

Sighing again, she turned to go back to bed —then her gaze was riveted to the table.

There had been the last few succulent dates saved from Christmas, and the last also of a particularly fine box of pears.

Looked forward to for the next day.

All that was left was a stalk and a few stones…

"Hmmm… hungry mouse! We shall see yet.."

She returned to bed—but not to sleep.

Sure enough, after a few minutes, there it was again. Scrabble, rustle.

This time Sister was very, very careful indeed. Very quiet as Nuns can be…

When she reached the sitting room, she held her breath and snapped on the light…

And there was a long, long, brown furry tail vanishing up the chimney... a swift, terrified backward glance from large nocturnal eyes…

"Oh, WOW!"

In the hearth, an apple, toothmarked, obviously dropped in the hasty flight.

Whatever was it? The size of a cat… Small wonder her furry ones had refused to face it…

Intrigued, Sister booted up the laptop and went online….. It took but a minute to identify this new resident as a pine marten.

That tail and face were unmistakable.

Rare, shy, rarely seen… Loners, as she was. They only came together in August to mate, and like badgers and seals, with a delayed implantation…

So this one was almost certainly a female, and pregnant?

And very territorial... so the hermitage was hers… she was here first.

Ahhh… Sister's heart was engaged now…

How best to support and nurture this shy creature, so hungry she had braved a human dwelling where cats lived.

Thoughtfully, she made a hot drink and returned to her bed—leaving the apple in the hearth… It was after five now, almost time for early prayers…

And as she lit the candles, she gave deep thanks for the trust of this shy nocturnal creature.

It was the beginning of a magical time for Sister. At the worst and most depressing time of year, the growing relationship between the shy pine marten and the Nun lifted her heart.

Aware of the possible danger to the cats if they got too bold, she left netting at the hearth at night… Putting food there behind it, and at the door for a few nights, until the food at the door started to vanish… Her early nights meant that the hearth cooled during the night…

The preferred diet was fascinating. Seemingly pine martens were blamed for egg thefts from hen runs—but eggs were left untouched. Fruit and bread were the favourites. She avoided meat because of the competition with the cats…

It became a last, joyous task before Compline, the last Office of the day, to put out food for the wild one. Knowing that by the time she rose again, the shy, needy creature would have run to the doorstep and feasted there in the night silence.

Early February saw snow and heavy frost. And almost every night of that harshest spell, Sister would be woken in the night by a frantic scrabbling at the skylight above her bed... and there she would be, belly now noticeably swollen, just scratching at the glass...

Not for food, as she had that... and that window was not part of her trodden path... Seemingly for the contact with another living creature?

Sister had made contact with others who knew and loved these timid creatures, but none had ever behaved like this.

So she lay there, watching her night visitor, wondering and awed.

Somehow, in the business and longer light of April, and with the increase of more natural food, Sister tailed off the feeding...

Then, one day, in full daylight, she was sitting knitting at the door when the pine marten appeared, on the wall just feet from Sister.

Sister was startled. There seemed no fear in the shy one. She simply sat and gazed at Sister.

And Sister saw how thin and haggard she looked, and her heart smote her. She was nursing; and finding food must be hard.

Quietly she went in and fetched an apple and two thick slices of bread.

There was no way she would shame this wild one by making her eat from her hand.

So Sister laid the food down by the doorstep and went back inside…

When a bare minute later, she glanced back, the bread had gone… And when she appeared at the door, the pine marten was on the stone wall again, bread in her mouth, waiting and watching until Sister appeared again. A long, intense look, then she was gone through the trees… and to Sister's horror as she went, a pair of magpies dive-bombed her, trying to steal the food.

Sister yelled at the birds, protected the pine marten thus until she disappeared into an impenetrable thicket.

And this was repeated twice more until all the food was gone.

Never again did Sister neglect to leave food out… such need to emerge in full light and appeal thus.

And although she knew now where the litter nested, never did she encroach on the privacy of the mother. Rather she avoided going near that thicket and if she had to, spoke loudly...

116

Never again did she see the pine marten face to face. Sometimes in the late afternoon, a furry form that was not a cat would shadow through the trees… and Sister would smile.

Until August and a wet, weary month.

Sister was indoors, but with the door open, reading by a small fire when the cats sat up, ears alert.

And in through the door ran a young pine marten, a small version of its mother… Unafraid, curious, it ran all round the room… the cats watched simply.

And often after that this was so… Just sometimes a young one in and out… Or glimpsed as a shadow in the trees in the late afternoon.

Part of the life of the hermitage, cherished and protected.

Chapter Eight

Sister took the alder catkins to the oratory, and they adorned the small altar in a glass of water…

This room was the heart of the hermitage, the place of prayer.

Simply furnished, always flowers or twigs there…

Silent and holy.

Now it was time for Vespers... quiet evening tide prayers as night approached.

And then her simple evening meal… toast made on the glowing turf fire, cheese, fruit, milk…

Enough for the night hours.

The cheese shared with one of the cats.

And she settled then by the fire, stitching her finished work up in the silence.

The cats came to her then.

These twin ones, saved and loved.

Two More Waifs

There had always been cats.

Living as Sister did in the wild places, they were a necessity, as mice and rats and the tiny voles abounded and were swift to make inroads into house and outbuildings where food was stored.

There had always been cats—and Sister thought back over the cavalcade of these sweet creatures in her years alone.

There had always been cats—and the saddest thing is that cats do not live for ever...

Always partings—and always incomings.

For like many cultures that had fought for survival until the last few decades, cats have still low priority in Ireland.

It had been the same on the island. They had no financial value, so money was never spent on them. They were counted as just above the vermin they controlled.

And when people moved, they left the cats behind, so a serious feral cat population exploded.

Many fed these outdoor cats, who after three generations became a breed apart. Often inbred, wary, bold when food was to be had.

Gradually this would change, and cat rescue folk were working hard to neuter ferals and persuade those who had cats to get them fixed.

Yet always there were cats needing homes; from tiny kittens to butch adults…

When Sister lost her old cat, she sought more then.

To be without was unthinkable.

Not as replacements, for nothing can ever replace a beloved pet, but as creatures needing a home, who would love and be loved for who they were.

So that was how these siblings came to her.

Abandoned at around three months, they were well-grown and used to people.

Obviously well cared for and well fed.

And as they needed to stay together, together Sister took them both, gladly.

She had a few short hours with them following her round the land, the female, Amanda, racing up a tree; the male, Caro, a little more sedate—before the realization came that these were sickening for some disease.

They would not eat. Not cat food, not tuna, not a scrap would they touch. And by morning, it was clear that they had at some stage on their progress through a cat rescue programme been infected with feline enteritis.

The nearest vet was over 30 miles away, and they would not have thanked Sister for bringing this disease to their surgeries.

And it was not the first time she had encountered this, so she knew what to do.

Days and nights passed in a blur as she fought to keep the kittens hydrated. Caro was amenable as he was by far the sicker of the two, but Amanda fought her.

And Sister learned to pretend to walk past the small cat with the syringe of rehydration fluid in her hand, then pounce swiftly and squirt it down the pink throat before the kitten knew what was happening.

The day she found Caro hiding in a box in the garden with that defeated look of death in his golden eyes, Sister drove the distance to the surgery and begged the vet nurse for help.

She was warned that after this length of time she would probably lose both youngsters – but she came away with a bottle of magic pink gloop.

And had the great joy to see Caro eating his gleeful way through a large saucer of cat food, until he could hardly move and lay purring on Sister's lap.

Sister lost neither kitten; they recovered at a great rate once that corner was turned... she gave the credit to prayer of course.

And to see them start to play and race round like the young creatures they were was a healing for her.

They were so different from each other… Caro was calmer, less emotional, more calculating. Amanda was a wild one…

Sister had forgotten how much time and energy young cats took up.

And these two!

Seeing them running up and down the hermitage roof and peering down the chimneys...

Catching Caro about to anoint a newly planted patch in the vegetable patch…

One day, Sister thought the magpies must have returned to the tall ash tree that towered over the hermitage. There was an old nest there… the flash of black and white caught her eye…

Then to her horror she realized it was Amanda. There was the little black and white face peering down at her as she lay in wait for any passing bird…

Sister prayed a prayer, then went back into the hermitage, unable to watch.

And some time later, the little cat sauntered in through the open door.

This one was an overt hunter. Both cats were utterly devoted to Sister now, and she learned to look and search before she sat down or got into bed.

Dead birds, or feathers, and once even a dead frog… All gifts of great affection. Hidden under a cushion or between the sheets…

Sister appreciated that this was simply their nature, and gave up feeding the birds then. Or fed them when the cats were asleep indoors and the doors closed on them.

But sometimes seeing Amanda race past with a bird in her mouth was just too much.

"OK, little one," as she gave chase. "I know it is your nature, but that does not mean I have to approve of it or support it. It is my nature to love these birds…"

But, too late.

The tiny bird Amanda dropped in her alarm lay inert and crumpled on the grass…

A robin. One of the most pathetic sights ever is a dead robin… tiny, brave scrap of scarlet, glorious voice stilled for ever… and those thread-thin legs all curled up…

Sister bent to gather the frail corpse in her tender hands… mourning the tiny songster and planning to bury it where no cat could do any more to it…

Then suddenly she realized that there was a bright, beady eye looking up at her… Then the bird moved, righted itself, and, as she opened startled hands, off it flew to safety.

Sister knew great satisfaction that day…

And now, these young cats were her devoted ones. As all rescued critters are that have known care…

Their fur was long and soft and shining, their golden eyes clear and alert…

Wild creatures with night hours around them, then soft pet-ones in day time.

They gathered on her lap now as the fire glowed and flamed in the evening stillness… purring, loving…

Just two more waifs safe.

There is of course no ending now… Life is continuous… critters come and go, seeking, finding, needing, caring… all these go on and on.

These have no end…

There is thus no ending now… just more beginnings…

Tales gathered in the gloaming by the
fireside when memory is bright and warm…

Printed in the United Kingdom
by Lightning Source UK Ltd.
126375UK00001B/22-96/P